Smithsonian

CURIOUS

ABOUT

FOSSILS

by Kate Waters

GROSSET & DUNLAP

An Imprint of Penguin Random House

For Lynette, avid beachcomber—KW

GROSSET & DUNLAP

Penguin Young Readers Group
An Imprint of Penguin Random House LLC

Smithsonian

Smithsonian Enterprises:
Christopher Liedel, President
Carol LeBlanc, Senior Vice President, Education and Consumer Products
Brigid Ferraro, Vice President, Education and Consumer Products
Ellen Nanney, Licensing Manager
Kealy Gordon, Product Development Manager

Smithsonian National Museum of Natural History:
Mike Brett-Surman, PhD, Museum Specialist for Fossil Dinosaurs, Reptiles, Amphibians, and Fish

----

PHOTO CREDITS: DORLING KINDERSLEY: 22 (top, photo by Francisco Gasco; bottom, photo by
John Temperton). LIBRARY OF CONGRESS: 10 (bottom). SMITHSONIAN NATIONAL MUSEUM OF NATURAL
HISTORY: front and back cover (fossils), 1, 3 (left), 4 (right, bottom), 5 (bottom left), 7, 9, 10 (top), 11, 12, 14–21, 24–32.
THINKSTOCK: cover (background, photo by somnuk), 3 (background, photo by somnuk; top, photo by Aysunbk; right,
photo by Jeff Chiasson), 4 (left, photo by Ca2hill), 5 (top left, photo by DC_Colombia, right, photo by AwakenedEye),
6 (photo by Prapann). WELLCOME LIBRARY, LONDON: 8 (bottom). WIKIMEDIA COMMONS / DMITRY BOGDANOV /
CC-BY-SA-3.0: 23 (background extended)

Library of Congress Cataloging-in-Publication Data is available.

ISBN 978-0-448-49019-9   10 9 8 7 6 5

Can you see a shape in this rock?

How about that one?

Whose tooth is this?

All these things are

FOSSILS.

(And that's a T.rex tooth!)

Let's find out what fossils
can tell us about life on Earth.

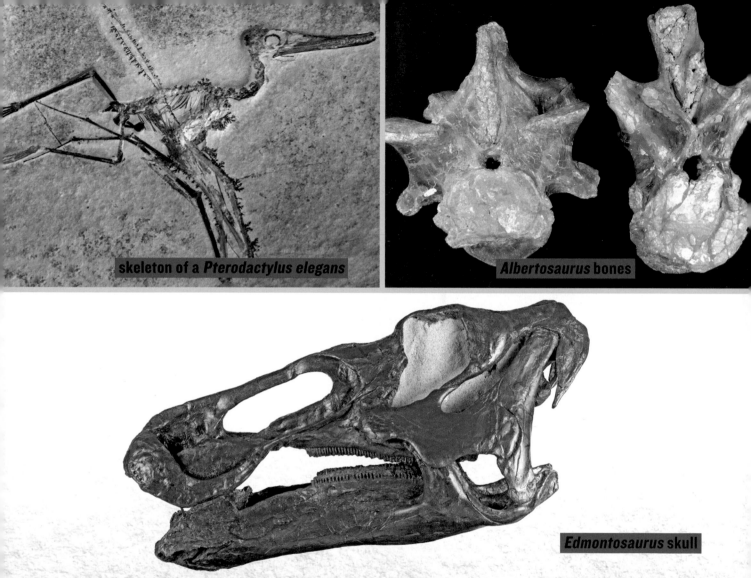

skeleton of a *Pterodactylus elegans*

Albertosaurus bones

Edmontosaurus skull

Fossils are evidence of life from the past. They give us clues about animals and plants that lived on Earth long ago.

Some fossils were part of an animal or a plant. They can be bones, shells, teeth, tree trunks, and other hard parts of living things. Fossils can also be tracks and traces left by animals.

mold fossil

insects in resin

tree fossil or petrified wood

Other fossils are like a mold. The object has **decayed**, but its shape remains.

Sometimes animals are trapped in tree **resin**. It hardens around them.

Even a tree can harden into rock!

It takes many thousands of years for a fossil to form. When a plant or animal dies on land or in water, **sediment** slowly covers it. Sediment can be sand, mud, silt, or clay. Sediment builds up on top of the animal or plant remains. It gets heavier and heavier. The layer below, where the animal or plant came to rest, turns to rock. Either the hard part of the plant or animal or its shape is now captured in the rock.

After many years, the layers of sediment slowly erode. Fossils appear. An earthquake can also **expose** fossils. So can construction work on buildings and tunnels.

sediment builds up

rock layers in Texas

marine animal fossils in a desert in Chile, South America

Fossils help tell about creatures that lived long ago. And that can mean big discoveries! In the nineteenth century, most people did not know dinosaurs had once existed. Mary Anning lived in England then. She was a curious girl from a poor family.

Mary Anning (1799–1847)

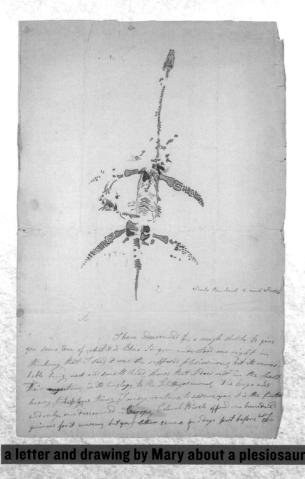

a letter and drawing by Mary about a plesiosaur

Mary looked for things along the seashore that she could sell. She picked up shells and colorful pebbles and rocks with shapes in them. If Mary saw something interesting in a rock, she carefully chipped it out with a hammer. At the time, all these finds were called "curiosities."

Plesiosaurus macrocephalus fossil

Scientists came to the Anning family shop to buy Mary's curiosities. From them, she learned about ancient animals and plants. Mary discovered several new kinds of prehistoric animals, including the first pterosaur ever found in England. Mary's brother, Joseph, found a huge skull. Together they dug out the rest of the skeleton of an ichthyosaur.

Ichthyosaurus fossil

Mary Anning looked at shapes to identify animals that lived long ago. In France, Georges Cuvier looked at fossils and compared them to animals that lived in his day. He looked for what was the same and what was different.

Georges Cuvier, right (1769–1832)

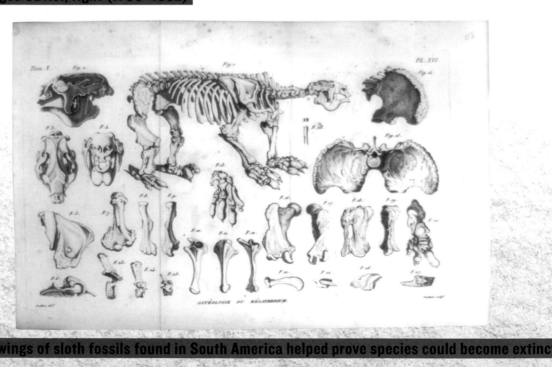

Cuvier's drawings of sloth fossils found in South America helped prove species could become extinct

Cuvier thought that some creatures must have disappeared or become **extinct**. He had discovered a skeleton of a mosasaur, a swimming reptile. He knew creatures like it were no longer alive anywhere. Cuvier believed a huge disaster must have happened on Earth to destroy living things like the mosasaurs. This was the first time that people considered **extinction**.

fossils of mosasaur skeleton, skull, and teeth

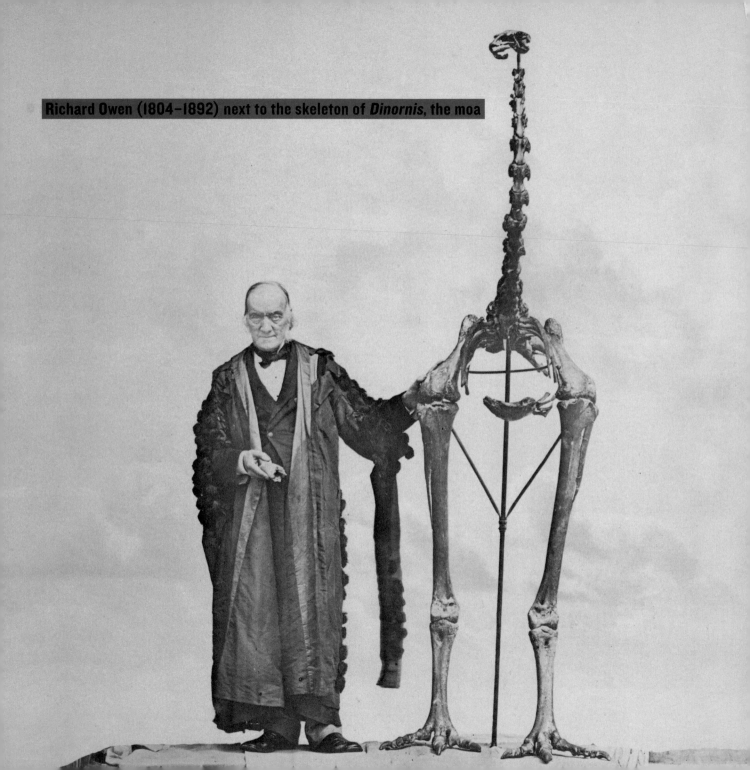

Richard Owen (1804–1892) next to the skeleton of *Dinornis*, the moa

Owen-Hawkins dinosaur models at the Crystal Palace in London (1854)

a hadrosaur model by Hawkins (1807–1894)

The word *dinosaur* was introduced by an English scientist, Sir Richard Owen. It means "fearfully great, a lizard." (Later, people realized that dinosaurs are not lizards.)

Owen studied to be a medical doctor but became interested in animals. When an animal died at the London Zoo, he was allowed to take it apart and study it. Owen used what he learned to look at fossils of bones and teeth from animals that lived long ago. This helped him imagine what those animals might have looked like.

Owen worked with an English sculptor, Benjamin Waterhouse Hawkins. They built the first life-size dinosaur models.

More and more fossil discoveries were made from the mid-1800s on. In New York, Othniel Charles Marsh collected rocks and trilobites when he was a boy. Ancient birds became his special interest. Marsh developed the idea that prehistoric birds such as *Ichthyornis* and *Hesperornis* were descended from dinosaurs. Today, his **theory** is considered fact.

crocodile fossils found by
Othniel Charles Marsh (1831–1899)

drawing of T.rex skeleton

Barnum "Mr. Bones" Brown hunted fossils for the American Museum of Natural History in New York. He found hundreds, including the very first *Tyrannosaurus rex* skeleton.

Barnum Brown (1873–1963)

Hesperornis skeleton

Charles Doolittle Walcott also grew up in New York and was a fossil collector when he was young. Later, Walcott found the famous fossil location in the Canadian Rockies called the Burgess Shale. Shale is a kind of rock. Walcott used dynamite to blast the rock apart. He mapped what fossils were found in the different rock layers.

Charles Walcott (1850–1927) at the Burgess Shale

Walcott's field diary

Charles Walcott was a paleobiologist. The scientific study of life on our planet using fossils as clues is called **paleontology**. "Paleo" means ancient.

Paleobiologists study ancient life forms or **organisms**. They usually work with animals.

paleobotanists and a fossil find

Paleobotanists study ancient plants, flowers, and trees.

Some fossils are so tiny that they can only be studied using microscopes by micropaleontologists.

using microscopes at Smithsonian's FossiLab

twentieth- and twenty-first-century paleontologists

Like all scientists, paleontologists look for answers to questions, such as:

What happened to the dinosaurs?
How do we know?

We now know that an asteroid, not a comet like the one shown here, hit the Earth.

In the 1970s, Luis Alvarez, an American physicist, became interested in these questions. Fossil evidence showed that large dinosaurs once roamed the Earth. Then about sixty-six million years ago, they disappeared. Alvarez worked with his son to find out why. Their theory was that a comet or asteroid struck Earth. This caused an enormous cloud of dust to block the sun's rays from reaching Earth. Plants died, and so did the dinosaurs that ate them— and the meat-eating dinosaurs that ate *them*. Most scientists today accept the Alvarezes' asteroid-extinction theory.

But in science, more answers means more questions.

Matthew Carrano is a research scientist who works at the Smithsonian's National Museum of Natural History. He studies how life evolved before and after the mass extinction.

Matthew Carrano with *Triceratops* fossils

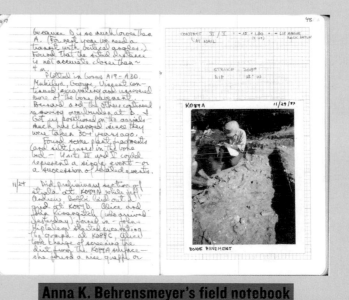

Anna K. Behrensmeyer's field notebook

The Smithsonian's Anna K. Behrensmeyer looks at what happens when a living thing dies. She researches why some living things become fossils and some don't.

Behrensmeyer at work

Gasosaurus

Dong Zhi-Ming, a paleontologist in China, is interested in what was living on our planet 170 million years ago. Not much is known about this period of time yet.

Zhi-Ming discovered a place in northwest China that has hundreds of fossils. Some had never been seen before. He has named more than twenty animals, including the ones shown here. *Shunosaurus* used the bony club on the end of its tail to bash its enemies.

Shunosaurus

Yangchuanosaurus

Paleontologists often travel by plane or jeep to remote places, searching for fossils.

a Smithsonian dinosaur expedition in Shell, Wyoming

When they find a good spot, the lead scientists must get permission to dig on the land. Then, they must raise money for equipment, food, and shelter for the dig crew. A dig crew is made up of scientists and students. Sometimes people volunteer to help, but they have to be ready to camp!

at a dig site

Today, paleontologists use computers in their work. But they also use many of the same tools that early fossil hunters did, including stone hammers and brushes.

If a dig crew finds a large fossil, paleontologists may use a drill or a pickax and chisel to carefully separate the fossil from a larger rock.

They make detailed drawings of what the fossil looks like in the rock. That way they know the original location of all the fossil parts. Then, very slowly, they begin to chip away at the rock surrounding the fossil. When most of the rock is gone, they use small picks, brushes, and even toothbrushes to remove the dust and rock bits. Photographs are taken at every stage.

When the fossil has been safely removed, it is packed up carefully. It will be sent to a university or museum for further study. Hopefully, a truck can make it to the dig site. If not, then the fossil crates are pushed and pulled on sleds until they can be more easily transported.

Whole fossil skeletons are rarely found. Most fossils are bits and pieces that have to be put together like a puzzle. But each small bit is saved. It might be the missing piece of a bigger skeleton already discovered!

preparation tools

wrapping up a fossil

a fossil field jacket

bits of *Stegosaurus* bone

Here are some interesting fossils that have been unearthed.

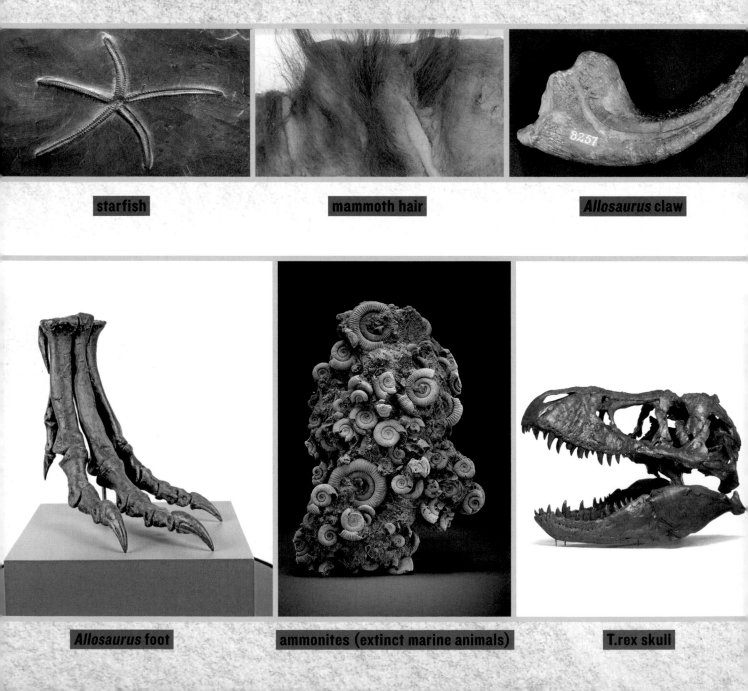

starfish

mammoth hair

Allosaurus claw

Allosaurus foot

ammonites (extinct marine animals)

T.rex skull

giant sloth poop

dinosaur eggs

GLOSSARY

decayed: broken down over time and fallen apart

expose: to show something that was covered up

extinct: when an entire species disappears from the Earth

extinction: an event when all of one type of living thing dies off

marine: having to do with the sea or ocean

organism: a life-form

paleontology: the study of life on Earth using fossils

petrified wood: dead wood that has turned into stone

resin: a liquid found in some trees and plants

sediment: sand, mud, silt, or clay

theory: ideas about how something works based on testing and proving those ideas

The Skeleton Inside You

by Philip Balestrino
illustrated by True Kelley

Revised Edition

HarperCollins*Publishers*

For my mother, Lillian Balestrino,
and for Fred Haynes —P.B.

For the children of Warner, New Hampshire
—T.K.

The *Let's-Read-and-Find-Out Science* book series was originated by Dr. Franklyn M. Branley, Astronomer Emeritus and former Chairman of the American Museum–Hayden Planetarium, and was formerly co-edited by him and Dr. Roma Gans, Professor Emeritus of Childhood Education, Teachers College, Columbia University. Text and illustrations for each of the books in the series are checked for accuracy by an expert in the relevant field. For more information about Let's-Read-and-Find-Out Science books, write to HarperCollins Children's Books, 10 East 53rd Street, New York, NY 10022. Manufactured in China.

HarperCollins®, ♨®, and Let's Read-and-Find-Out Science® are trademarks of HarperCollins Publishers Inc.

Library of Congress Cataloging-in-Publication Data
Balestrino, Philip.
  The skeleton inside you / by Philip Balestrino ; illustrated by True Kelley.—Rev. ed.
     p.   cm. — (A Let's-read-and-find-out science book)
  "A Harper Trophy book"
  (A Let's-read-and-find-out book)
  Summary: An introduction to the human skeletal system, explaining how the 206 bones of the skeleton join together, how they grow, how they help make blood, what happens when they break, and how they mend.
  1. Human skeleton—Juvenile literature. [1. Skeleton. 2. Bones.] I. Kelley, True, ill. II. Title. III. Series.
QM101.B35   1989   88-24600
611—dc19   CIP
ISBN 0-06-445087-2 (pbk.)   AC

Published in hardcover by HarperCollins Publishers.
First Harper Trophy edition, 1989.
12 13 SCP 20 19 18

The Skeleton Inside You

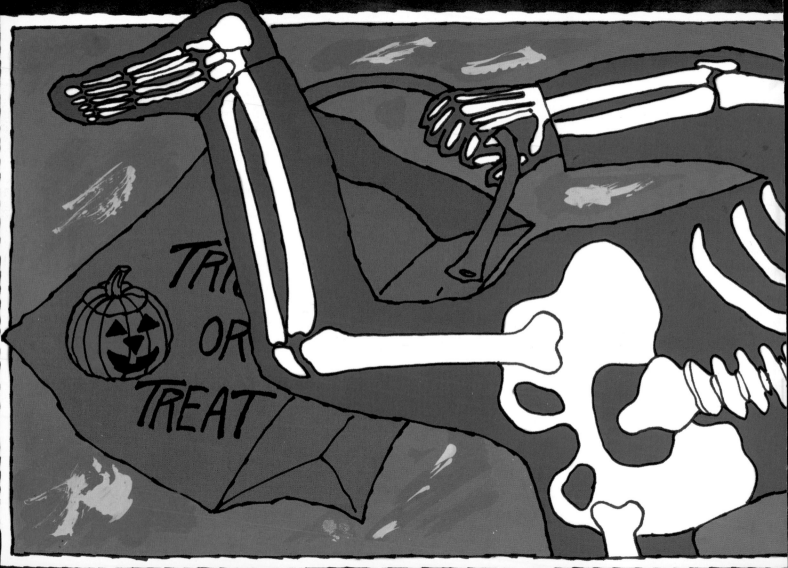

On Halloween I wore a skeleton costume. I used to think skeletons were made up just to scare people. Now I know that skeletons are real. They are not scary. I would not be me without a skeleton. You would not be you.

Skeletons are made up of many bones. Bones give you shape. A ball of clay has no bones inside it. You can make a ball of soft clay into any shape you want. You can make it into a little figure. Then you can squash the figure and roll it into a mustache or a snake. But nothing can change your shape, because you have a skeleton inside you.

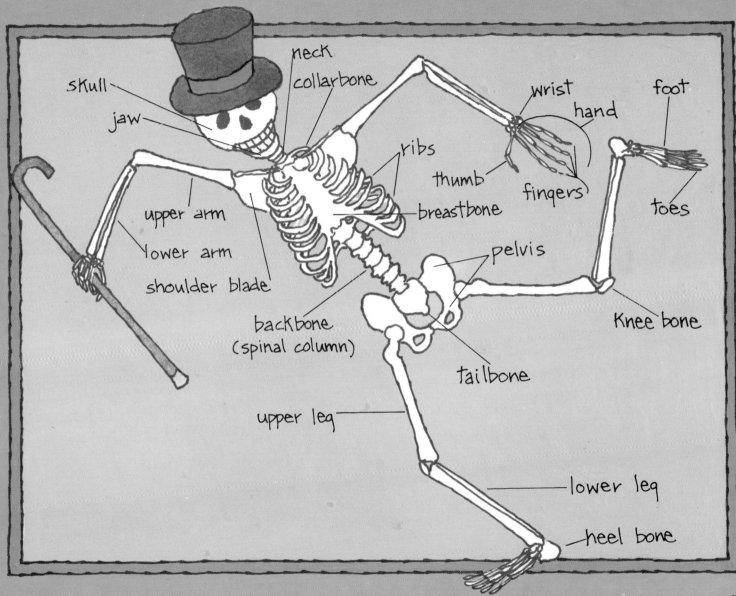

skull

jaw

neck

collarbone

wrist

hand

foot

ribs

thumb

fingers

breastbone

toes

upper arm

lower arm

shoulder blade

pelvis

backbone
(spinal column)

knee bone

tailbone

upper leg

lower leg

heel bone

A marionette has a skeleton too, but it is made of wood and wire, not of real bones.

A plain wooden chair is like a skeleton without any covering. When the chair is covered with stuffing and cloth, it is like your skeleton covered with muscles and skin. But your skeleton is different. It is made up of bones.

Your skeleton is made up of 206 bones. There are 64 bones just in your two hands and arms. Some of your bones are big, others are small. Some bones are flat, others are round.

Bones are hard. They give your body shape. Your ears and nose have something called cartilage in them to give them shape. Cartilage is softer than bone, and so it can bend. When the barber folds over your ear to cut your hair, your ear does not break off. That's because of the soft cartilage in your ear.

Once I pushed my nose flat against a bakery window to look at some cookies. My nose didn't hurt, and it didn't break off. It came back to the same shape. Push your nose flat. It will bend too, because it has cartilage inside it.

Sometimes bones get broken. I fell out of a tree once and broke my arm. My mother took me to the doctor. The doctor took an X ray. Then he fitted the bone back together. Next the doctor put a stiff plaster cast on my arm to keep the bone together. I had a sling around my neck to hold my arm and the plaster cast. For several weeks I wore the cast. All the time, the bone was growing back together. When the doctor took off the plaster cast, my bone was all healed.

Bones live and grow, just like every other part of the body. Bones start to grow before you are even born. As your bones grow longer, you grow taller, until you're all grown.

(THE BONES IN YOUR HAND CHANGE AND GROW — JUST AS YOU DO!)

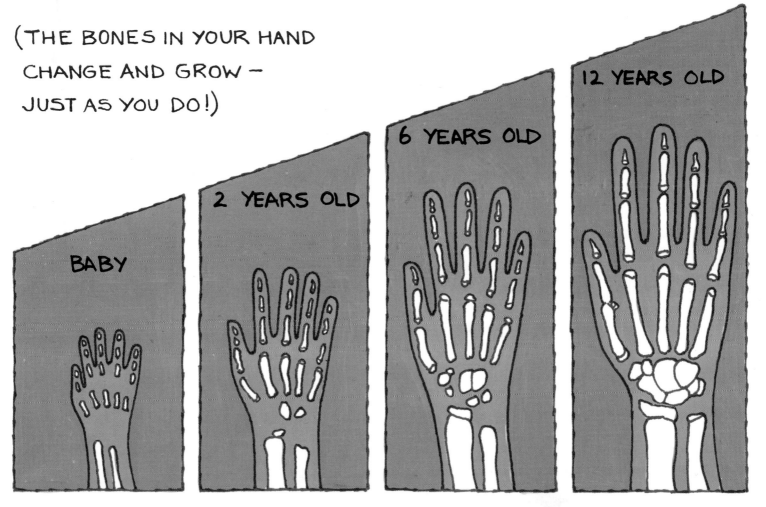

BABY

2 YEARS OLD

6 YEARS OLD

12 YEARS OLD

Foods like milk and cheese and some leafy vegetables have calcium in them. Calcium is a mineral that helps bones grow. Calcium also makes bones hard. Without it, all your bones would be as soft as cartilage. They would be soft enough to tie into knots.

The butcher cut up a big soup bone for my mother.
The inside of it looked like this:

It was a bone from a big steer's leg. Your leg bones
look almost the same inside.

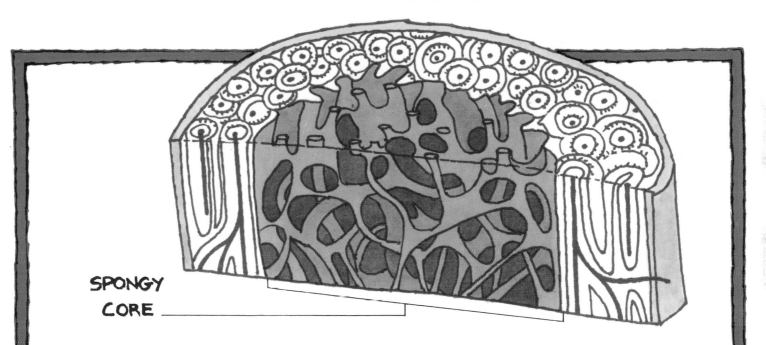

SPONGY CORE

Inside your bones is a core that looks something like a sponge. All the little spaces in the core are filled with soft bone marrow. Bone marrow helps make the red cells of your blood.

The insides of bones store calcium and other minerals that come from the food you eat. These minerals are saved up until your body needs them.

All your 206 bones fit together to make your skeleton.
Your skeleton helps you stand up straight.

Without a skeleton, you would be like a ball of soft clay that can be molded into anything. You would be as floppy as a big beanbag.

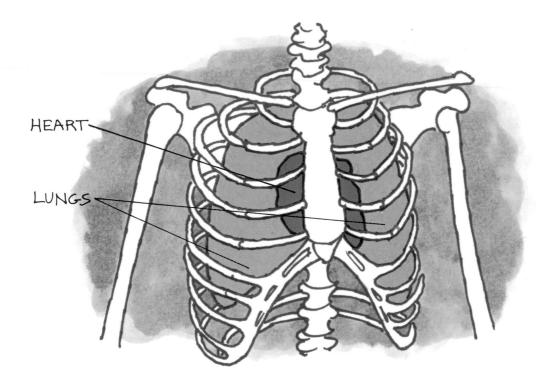

HEART

LUNGS

Some bones in your skeleton protect important parts
inside you. Your rib bones cover your heart and lungs.
Your skull protects your brain from hard knocks. The
bones around your eyes protect them the way a football
helmet does.

Your skeleton also helps you walk, run, and jump and move in many ways.

The bones of your skeleton fit together at joints.
Without joints, your skeleton could not move or bend.
Shoulders, elbows, and ankles are joints.

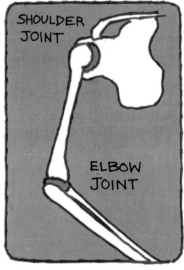

SHOULDER
JOINT

ELBOW
JOINT

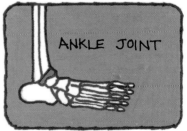

ANKLE JOINT

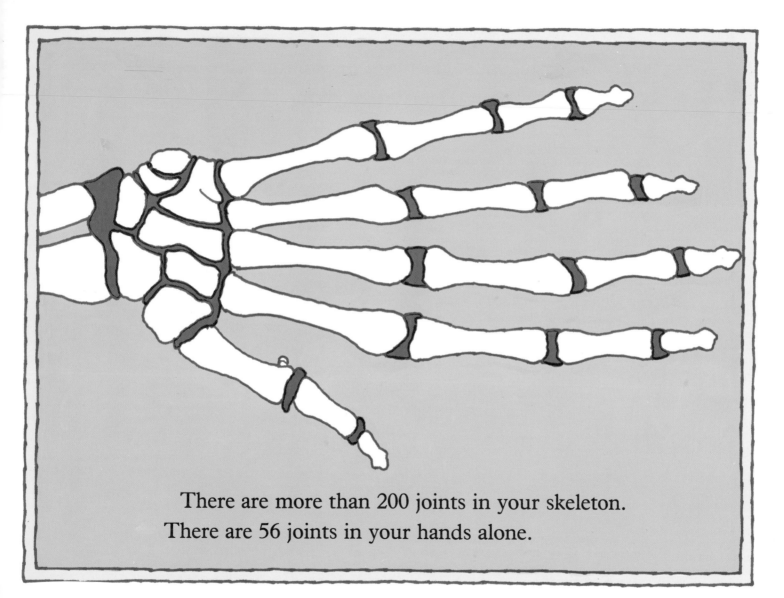

There are more than 200 joints in your skeleton.
There are 56 joints in your hands alone.

The bones are held at the joints by ligaments. Ligaments are like strong pieces of string. They hold the bones together at the joints. But they also slide back and forth and sideways to let the bones move.

KNEE

KNEE JOINT

LIGAMENTS

Your backbone is made up of 34 bones that fit together at 33 separate joints. That is why you can twist and turn almost any way. You can do a somersault. Or you can make yourself into a bridge, back up or belly up. If a backbone were only one bone, you could not do these things.

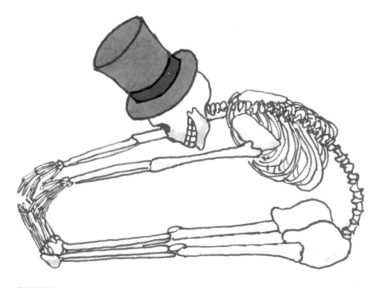

31

You could not put on a scary skeleton suit. You would not be able to run or jump or ring doorbells on Halloween if you did not have a skeleton inside you.